Introduction

Perhaps the title for this bo ˙   · it is
on these occasions, or short   these
excursions really excel. Crashing   ;ades
make for some exciting experience   days
are curtailed due to rainfall there i   r two
than exploring these spectacles.

Although the 250 foot high Pi _ _ghest
waterfall in Wales there are three falls which exceed that height in this area
– Maesglase, Pistyll y Llyn and Rhaeadr y Cwm. All these have a mighty 600
foot drop. Pistyll y Rhaeadr is easily approached by car and is then a very
short walk to view this majestic fall. Although there are paths up the side
the best view is from the base. Note the arch low down which the water has
created and now forces its way through. The fall is located near to the village
of Llanrhaeadr-ym-Mochnant, between Oswestry and Lake Vyrnwy.

Other magnificent waterfalls, not described here although it is possible
to drive to them, are at Devil's Bridge, 12 miles east of Aberystwyth on the
A4120. A £2.50 charge is levied to access the trail to view these 300 foot falls
in a narrow ravine that has been carved out by the fast flowing river – the Afon
Mynach. This river joins the Afon Rheidol some 400 feet lower down. Well
worth the journey.

Many of the waterfalls described in this book also lie in some of the most
beautiful woodlands in Wales. Some of the walks follow rough and slippery
ground – especially when approaching the falls – *so do take care.* All the
waterfalls described can be viewed from safe ground. A few, however, have
ledges or narrow paths to walk along to get better views. DO NOT go along
these unless you are confident and sure footed. *A slip into a turbulent torrent
will inevitably be fatal.*

Whilst none of the walks described venture high into the mountains you
are nevertheless in mountainous terrain. As such appropriate clothing and
supportive footwear are required. When walking through farmland where
there are sheep (*you are in Wales!*) please keep your dog on a lead, and always
adhere to the Country Code.

Although there are some longer walks in this book the majority are
reasonably short and are thus suitable for all levels of fitness. I hope you have
as much enjoyment in discovering these falls as I have.

Oh, and *enjoy* the rain (if it comes)!!

WALK I

MAESGLASE

DESCRIPTION This is a gentle walk to a dramatic and little known 600 feet high waterfall with one section of the fall over 200 feet in a single drop. 2 miles allow 1¼ hours.

START At a small pull in off the narrow road by the side of the Nant Maesglase.

DIRECTIONS From Machynlleth take the A489 towards Newtown. At the roundabout in Cemmaes Road turn left on the A470 towards Dolgellau. Drive through Dinas Mawddwy where, ¾ miles from the speed de-restriction sign, a left turn – unsigned – leads along the narrow lane until it possible to park your car off the road on your right just before crossing the Nant Maesglase. There are some recycling bins on your left just after you have turned left.

I Walk back up the rise to a track which branches off on your right. Follow this a few metres and pass through a gate. Continue along the level green track to the next gate. Go through this and continue along the track keeping a conifer plantation on your left. At the end of the plantation there is a stile to the left of a gate. Climb over the stile and continue along the less defined track to a ruined mine building – boggy along here, so keep high for the drier part!

2 Continue climbing gently ahead for 200m past a smaller ruin to the end of a small spoil heap on your left. A vague path leads off to your right here. Follow this down to a stream. Cross this to the left hand, upper corner of a small conifer plantation. Keep the plantation to your right and in a few metres a stile is crossed into a field. Fifty yards further on cross a ditch and walk half right down and along a step in the field to a gate. Go through the gate on your left and walk down

the edge of the field with the fence to your right. Walk through a gate on your right to join a stony track. Follow this down – *there is a great view of Maesglase waterfall here* – to a gate. Pass through this and walk down a cutting to the gate immediately before the Nant Maesglase.

3 Go through the gate and ford the shallow stream – this may be impossible after prolonged rainfall – to join a track. Turn right and walk along the track to a gate. Go through this and continue to the next one just before reaching Ty'n-y'braich. Pass through this and continue along the track, passing below the house, to another gate. Go through this to join a tarmac road and follow it down back to your car.

*There is a **memorial** stone to Hugh Jones by the road side at the start of the track. Translated, the inscription is – 'Not far from Ty'n-y-braich on this road stands the ruin of Maesglasau, the home of Hugh Jones, the Hymnist 1749 – 1825'.*

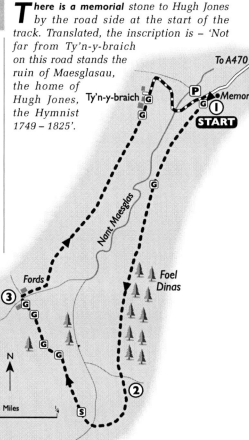

WALK 2

DYFI FURNACE WATERFALL

DESCRIPTION A very short, easy walk, mainly on quiet lanes but a good one giving expansive views of the Dyfi Estuary. 2 miles, 1 hour.

START At the car park for Dyfi Furnace

DIRECTIONS From Machynlleth follow the A487 towards Aberystwyth. Drive over the bridge spanning the Afon Einion in Furnace and turn right immediately to drive down into the car park.

1 Rejoin the road and turn left over the bridge admiring the fine fan shaped waterfall. A path leads down to the river in a few yards. Admire, too, the fine waterwheel. Back on the road walk 100 yards beyond the bridge in the Machynlleth direction and turn right up the lane beyond the houses. The lane rises and levels out. Continue to a cattle grid. Go over this and take the path on your left that slants up the hill. An arrow points the way. Join the lane again and follow it up and around a hairpin bend to a seat. *Here are fine views of the Dyfi Estuary.* Keep on the road for 500 yards. After a slight descent take the smaller lane at the footpath sign on your right.

2 Follow this down to a cottage. Just before it go right through a gate and down the path through trees to a bridge. Cross over and go through a gate. Climb the path to the right to meet the lane which is followed into Furnace. Turn right to the car park.

Dyfi Furnace

WALK 3

AFON DULAS & FOEL FRIOG

DESCRIPTION This is a woodland, hill and valley walk giving lovely views across to Cadair Idris and down into Aberllefenni a village with a long history of slate mining. There are some small, though attractive, waterfalls on the Afon Dulas before commencing the valley section of the walk and another fall before joining the road in the village. The walk follows red markers throughout. 2 miles, 1½ hours.

START At the Foel Friog Forest Enterprise car park immediately before the sign for Aberllefenni village.

DIRECTIONS Take the A487 from Machynlleth towards Dolgellau. At the village of Corris and almost opposite the Braich Goch Bunk House/pub turn right into the village and continue along this minor road to the car park on your right just before the village sign for Aberllefenni.

1 From the car park walk downstream – there are walk signs here – to join a narrow road. Turn left over the bridge. *Just to your right here there are the remains of the old narrow gauge railway that once transported the slate from Aberllefenni to Machynlleth and the port of Derwenlas. It was built in 1859 and closed finally in 1948 although parts of it are now being restored.* Walk along the track ignoring one that goes off to your right and continue up to a finger post indicating a bridleway on your right 50 yards further on. Turn up to your right here – marker post and red arrow. Follow the path which gradually becomes steeper to a marker post. Bear left here and follow the much steeper path through larch and in spring a wonderful carpet of bluebells to a junction and marker post. Turn right here up the track – an old drovers route – to some ruins – Pen y Bryn. *This is a fine example of a Welsh farmstead. It was*

a traditional longhouse having the family dwelling at one end, animals in the middle with bedding and fodder for the animals at the other.

2 Bear left at the marker post by the ruins and again go uphill to reach an undulating path through conifers – *which were planted in 1978. There are great views across to Cadair Idris, down into the valley and Aberllefenni.* Continue along this lovely section to a marker post. Bear left along a level green path to reach another marker post. Turn left here to follow the path down through a conifer avenue and then more steeply through broadleaf woodland and native Welsh sessile oak trees to a marker post. Bear right and descend to join a wide path by a gate above the river. To obtain good views of the waterfalls below, turn right for 50 yards or so. Return to the gate.

3 Go through the gate and walk along the wide level path to a marker post by a ruin. Turn right to go over the stile and continue along and around the right edge of the field passing a marker post and wide gate to your right to another marker post by a smaller gate on your right. Go through this and continue along the stony path and grassy continuation to a marker post and stile. Climb over the stile. A few paces ahead walk across a footbridge spanning the Afon Dulas to a gate at the far side. Go through a further two gates and turn left to join a narrow tarmac road. Follow this up to cross a bridge on your left opposite the Plas. *There is a pretty waterfall here.* Climb up an old flight of slate steps on your right at the far side of the bridge to join the road. Turn left and walk past the modern dressing floor of the slate mine on your left – *and a fine row of Georgian Miners cottages to your right. Further on is an old flight of steps leading from the road to the old railway line and houses that are of more recent build.* Continue walking through the village back to your car.

4

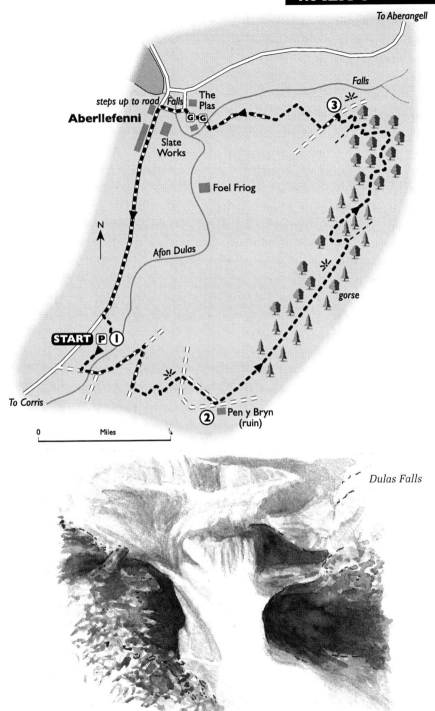

To Aberangell

Falls

steps up to road / *Falls*

Aberllefenni

The Plas

③

G G

Slate Works

Foel Friog

N

Afon Dulas

gorse

START P ①

To Corris

② Pen y Bryn (ruin)

0   Miles   ¼

Dulas Falls

PISTYLL Y LLYN

DESCRIPTION This is an extremely scenic walk. It initially follows the level valley floor of Cwmrhaiadr before tackling the steep hillside alongside the waterfall. This is followed by a short section through conifers before descending along a broad ridge with fantastic views towards the Arans, Cadair Idris and the Tarrens. There are some boggy sections. The path up to the top of the fall is narrow, steep, exposed and very slippery in places. **EXTREME CARE** is needed and this section is certainly not advised in icy conditions. 4½ miles, 3 hours.

START At the road junction before Cwmrhaiadr farm.

DIRECTIONS From Machynlleth take the A487 towards Aberystwyth. After 1½ miles a sign to Glaspwll indicates where you make a left turn onto the minor road. Follow this road to Glaspwll. At the phone box on your right bear left along the narrower road for 1½ miles to where cars may be parked on the roadside allowing other traffic to pass. There are signs here indicating that cars are not permitted any further down either of the roads.

1 Walk down the road then up to Cwmrhaiadr farm. A sign ahead indicates the way to the fall. Turn left and go up to and through a gate. Follow the track to a junction. Go left here, again signed to the falls. Bear right at the next junction by some hawthorn trees and follow the level track heading towards the fall which is seen ahead. Continue along to a gate. Go through this and keep walking along the level track to two gates. Ignore the left hand one and go ahead to a stile on the right of the other gate. Go over the stile and follow the level grassy path with a fence to your left. Continue to another stile. Climb over this where there are young trees planted and continue damply through them to a rusting gate. Clamber over this and continue along a drier grassy path to a rusting corrugated shed. There is an old spoil heap down to your right here.

2 The path rises gently from here and passes a fenced and tree lined shaft – *Cwmrhaiadr mine* – on your left and a hub of an old wheel on your right. Cross the stream and follow a steeper path up to a wide depression. Climb much more steeply up the left hand side of this and 100 yards before a clump of conifers drop into the depression and continue up to them. Follow an improvement of the path out to your right. The path becomes very well defined but is narrow. Keep following this rising line across the hillside with increasing exposure as height is gained – TAKE CARE HERE. The path eases near the top and becomes level once the top of the fall has been passed.

3 Head across to the bottom edge of a conifer plantation and go over the stile. Follow a quite distinct, but boggy path through the trees to a forest road. Turn left up this and continue for 150 yards to a right hand bend where a vague path on your left leads up a break between the trees. Keep following this break to the edge of the plantation where there is a stile. Go over this and walk half right to join a forest road. Turn left and continue down to a level section. A large concrete pipe marks the start of a narrow steep stream down to your left. Continue a further 50 yards to where a well marked path leads off to your left and joins a broad ridge.

4 Follow the ridge down passing a tiny but pretty pond on your left. Keep going down until almost at the bottom and in sight of a fence where wheel tracks enter from the right and pass over a small rocky area. Go half left here to a stile over the fence. Climb over and continue straight ahead – paths are absent now. Continue through a very dilapidated fence and continue to the next fence where a large gateway – the gate being defunct – is walked through. Pass to the left of a small wooden and barbed wire enclosure. *This at one time housed a TV aerial!!* Keep going down past a solitary wood post and keep heading down to wheel tracks and a grassy wall bank. Follow the sunken path down which in places is very heavily overgrown. The sunken path ends at a track junction. Go left to a gate and pass through this.

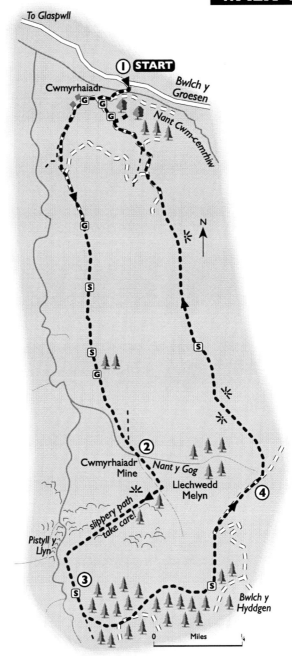

Continue down the grassy track to another gate. Go through this and bear left to pass some large conifers on your left to join the track of your outward journey at the farm. Turn right back to your car.

CWM RHEIDOL WATERFALLS

DESCRIPTION A gentle walk through woodland and along the bank of the Afon Rheidol, with a good view of The Stag! There are some particularly fine waterfalls to admire. 5½ miles, 3 hours.

START At the Cwm Rheidol Visitor Centre.

DIRECTIONS From Aberystwyth take the A44 towards Llangurig. Turn right in Capel Bangor just beyond the Tynllidiart Arms and continue along this minor road for 4 miles to the Visitor Centre.

which is just above river level, to another stile. Climb over this and continue along a rougher section until is possible to descend to a meadow on your left – marker post and white arrow at the edge of the field. Keeping to the edge of the meadow, walk towards the prominent green footbridge seen ahead. When level with this drop down to a stile on your left. Climb over and turn left – there is a picnic table to your right. *A grand place to have lunch!* Cross over to the middle of the bridge – to *admire the fine Rheidol Falls and return to the picnic site.*

2 Go back to the path and pass above the fish ladder and falls on your left to a stile. Go over this and follow the edge of the field close to the river. *Looking over to*

1 Walk out of the car park to the road and turn right. Walk past the picnic site on your left and continue to the turning for Aberffrwd. Turn left down this road and cross the Felin Newydd Bridge – *with the attractive Felin Newydd waterfalls below.* It is worth taking a slight detour to your left at the end of the bridge to the observation balcony to view the falls and 'The Stag' high up on the left hand side of the valley. Return to the road and continue up to a sharp right hand bend 100m ahead. Turn left here bypassing the, seemingly, redundant gate! Follow the track, which shortly passes a wooden bench on your left, to where it rises. On the left there is a level path – indicated by an arrow. Take this attractive path and continue to a stile. Climb over this and continue, to cross another. At a path junction keep to the lower path and follow it,

your left, just below the skyline, there is a fine waterfall – on the Nant Bwa-drain. From the first large mine building ruin on your right, part of the old Gwaith Goch mine, walk up to the fence above on your right. Go left along this to a stile. Climb over this and continue with the fence on your left along the level path. *A pretty waterfall is passed on your right before you reach a path junction.*

3 Ignore the right hand one and take the left hand level path. This quickly becomes a grassy track and goes up a small rise before it levels out once more as you walk through pretty woodland. Continue to a gateway with a ruined gate. Pass through this and continue to another gate. Go through this and continue along the level path to where a short rise again leads to a level section. Continue to where the path splits. Ignore the left hand lower bridleway and take the right hand steep grassy one. Continue up until a clearing gives you a great view of Rheidol

mine across the valley. Here a path leads down to your left. There is no marker for this but it is quite obvious. Continue down steeply to a stile on your left. Cross over this and continue down to a gate just before Pont Plwca footbridge. Go through the gate and cross over the footbridge to join the road. Turn right and walk upstream a few yards to admire the Upper Falls.

4 Your return walk is down the quiet road back to your car at the Visitor Centre.

The Vale of Rheidol Steam Railway

COED MAEN ARTHUR

DESCRIPTION This exquisite walk has some magical moments. Contorted rock features along the Ystwyth to fine woodland, there is plenty to marvel at. Although there are many way markers to guide you it can get confusing. 2½ miles, 2 hours.

START In Pont-rhydy-groes close to the Miners Arms Hotel.

DIRECTIONS From Aberystwyth take the A487 towards Cardigan and turn off on to the A4102 for Devils Bridge, then immediately turn right on to the B4340 – signed Trawsgoed. Drive through here and continue to Pont Llanafan. Immediately beyond the bridge turn left onto a minor road and continue to Pontrhydygroes. Car parking is close to the Miners Arms Hotel on the roadside.

I From Walk away from the Miners Arms along the B4343 to the road you have just driven out from. Turn right here and walk for 150m, passing Lisburne Motors on your right, to a finger post. Turn right here and walk through the kissing gate and follow the path down to another kissing gate. Go through this and keep following the fenced path to the spectacular Miners Bridge. Cross the bridge and walk up to a path junction. Go left here and follow the path up to a forest road. Go left along this at first slightly up then slightly down to a narrow path branching off to your left almost opposite a marker post. Descend this path past a marker post. Continue down some steps and walk along to cross a tiny footbridge to a sharp right hand bend by a marker post. Walk along the easy path – over another tiny footbridge – and continue close to the Afon Ystwyth. All too soon this magical section ends and the path climbs away from the river. At the top of the rise bear left along a level section above the river. (There is a scramble down part way along, to the river edge, where there are three logs laid across some trees. TAKE GREAT CARE if doing this as a slip would

have serious consequences). Keep following the level path to some steps which again take you away from the river and follow the easy path to your left at the top to join a forestry track.

2 Turn left along the track and left again almost immediately by a yellow way marker and follow the path slightly down then along. At the next marker post turn sharp left then sharp right at the next one a few metres further on. Follow the path past old mine workings to a short climb up to a marker post and continue up to a forestry track – marker post. Walk to your right for 20m to some steps on your left. Go up these and along to some more. Continue up quite steeply to more steps and a marker post where a grassy track is joined. Walk to your right for 30m to three steps on your left. Go up these and continue to an open area. Continue up a gradually rising path to some steps close to a stream on your left. (A small level path leads off from here to the stream, where there is a very fine ribbon waterfall).

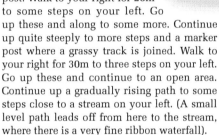

3 Return to the steps and continue steeply up past several more flights of steps to a marker post – *great views across the valley*. Turn left along the easy path to a marker post and path junction. Take the right hand path which is easy at first then steep walking to a level section after passing through an area of conifers. *There is a bench here to admire the view – and rest!* Continue easily through conifers to a stile. Go over this and continue half right along a narrow green path to a marker post. Swing sharply right and continue to a stile. Pass over this and follow the level path to a descent which leads to a marker post at a path junction. DO NOT follow the direction indicated on the marker post. Go sharp left along a level path then descend to a marker post on your right. Go left here and continue down to another marker post. Walk to your left again and arrive by a cottage on your left as the forest

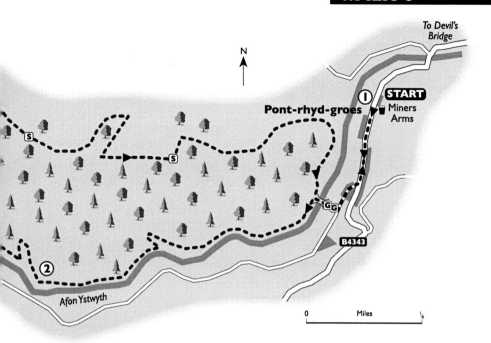

road is reached – marker post. Walk down the road to a marker post on your right. Opposite this to your left is a path. Follow the path down to the Miners Bridge. Cross over and continue back to your car in the village.

*T*he original **Miners Bridge** was built around 1850 but had disappeared through neglect by 1930. The present bridge was erected in 2002. 'Camau Lledr' (Thieves' Steps) – stepping stones – were used before the original bridge was erected.

Miners Bridge

11

WALK 7

THE HAFOD ESTATE WATERFALLS

DESCRIPTION This dramatic and at times exciting walk has some fantastic river scenery, dramatic waterfalls and woodland containing some amazing trees. This circular walk is well marked by different colour marker posts mentioned in the description. It takes in many of the fine features of the Hafod Estate. All in all, this a fantastic walk. Please note that there are some narrow and at times exposed paths on this walk demanding care. 4 miles, 3 hours.

START At the Hafod Estate car park on the B4574.

DIRECTIONS From Aberystwyth take the A487 towards Cardigan and turn off on to the A4120 for Devils Bridge, then immediately turn right on to the B4340 – signed Trawsgoed. Drive through here and continue on the B4343 to Pont Llanafan. Immediately beyond the bridge turn left onto a minor road and continue to Pontrhydygroes. Cross the bridge over the river and turn immediately right and continue on the B4574 to the car park on your right, near the church, in 1½ miles

I From the car park head towards a YELLOW marker post on the east side. Walk down the track to a marker post on your left where the track splits. Turn left along the path between conifers and continue to a stile. Go over this and walk along to a marker post on your right and a stile on your left. Now follow BLUE marker posts. Go down to your right to a stile which is crossed to enter a field. Follow the path across the field – marker posts – to a stile by a gate. Go over this and follow the path between 'Hawthorn Cottage and Pond'. Follow marker posts down the field to a track – marker post. Turn left for 50 metres, then walk half right to a RED marker post on a lower track. Turn left here down the right hand and even lower one. Continue down this track to a right hand bend and marker post on your left. Turn left

and follow the path down passing the 'Ice House' on your right to the 'Alpine Bridge'. Cross over and turn right along a path that leads to a RED ringed marker ahead. Red markers are now followed.

2 Turn left up the steep path on your left to a stile. Go over this to a marker post and continue up the hill, ignoring the viewpoint sign, to where the path levels. Just after this go over a stile and turn left – red arrow – and follow the path with a fence to your left to join a forest road. Turn left along this and follow it past a viewpoint on your left to a marker post on your right. Turn up to your right here away from the road and continue to the beautiful 'Mossy Seat' Falls. Cross the stream by the footbridge and follow the narrow path to 'The Tunnel'. Walk through this and continue passing a path coming up from your left. Keep going to reach a path/track junction. Cross straight over the track to a marker post, again ignoring the viewpoint sign. Continue around a knoll to a path junction where there is a slight clearing and a finger post nailed to a tree indicating the way to 'Cavern Cascade' as well as marker posts. Follow the narrowing path, alongside the Nant Gau, upstream. Ignore the footbridge down to your left, and continue up, passing an adit on your right. Keep going along this amazing path, passing a fine waterfall tumbling into the Nant Gau on the opposite side, to the entrance of the very impressive 'Cavern Cascade'.

3 Retrace your steps back to the clearing and continue downhill with the Nant Gau to your right to a stile. Go over this and follow the right edge of the field to another stile. Cross over this and turn right along the track to a track junction. Turn left and just before crossing the 'Pont Dologau' go through a small gate on your right. This part of the walk follows GREEN marker posts. Keep following the path above the Afon Ystwyth to pass by the remains of the 'Gothic Arch' just before the 'Chain Bridge'. Cross the bridge and follow the path steeply up to a track. Turn left along this and follow it to a footbridge spanning the top of the 'Peiran Falls'. Cross over. Keep walking along this track to

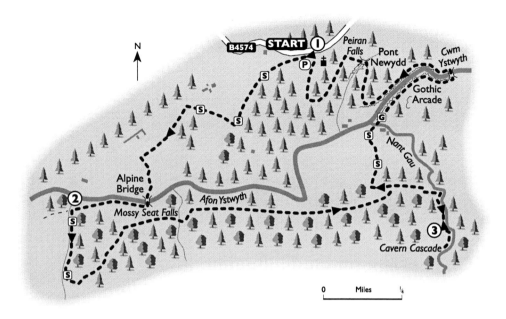

where a track on your left – BLUE marker – leads down to the 'Peiran Falls'. Retrace your steps a few yards to rejoin the forest track. Cross over this – BLUE marker here – and ascend the steep path passing the graveyard and church to your right into the car park.

About the author, Des Marshall

Des has had a lifelong interest in mountaineering, climbing, walking, canyoning and caving. As well as being an advisor, trainer and assessor in outdoor activities, he has undertaken many expeditions worldwide but now focuses more on local excursions. After moving away a couple of years ago, the lure of the plethora of exciting walking and climbing became too much and he now lives in Glantwymyn, near Machynlleth.

CRAIG Y PISTYLL, LLYN CRAIGYPISTYLL & LLYN SYFYDRIN

DESCRIPTION This is a superb walk. As well as being easy to follow it includes a fine waterfall, secluded lake and a sense of solitude. 5 miles, 3 hours.

START At the car park just above Llyn Pendam close to the junction with the turning to Ponterwyd.

DIRECTIONS From Aberystwyth take the A487 towards Machynlleth and turn right on to the A4159 immediately before entering Bow Street. Take the first left off this road – signed to Penrhyncoch. Turn left again at the next road junction and continue into the village. Turn right at the war memorial to your right and signed Pendam Mountain Road and Cwmsymlog. Follow this road to Llyn Pendam. Drive past the turning right to Ponterwyd. Almost immediately there is a turning to your left into the car park.

I Leave the car park by the obvious path leading up into the forest and continue along it until you reach a forestry track – marker post on your left for bikers! Go half left along a wide path to join a fence on your left. Walk down this path to a track (gate on your left). Turn right along the track to a way marker on your left after 200 yards. Turn left here and walk steeply down the path which initially goes through young conifers until they end. De-forestation has taken place beyond here and the mysterious forest has gone. It is now a wide open area with a clear path descending more gradually. Near the bottom a small clump of trees is seen rising above some ruins. Veer right to these and continue down to a flat area and a small stream. Cross this and continue to a grassy area. Turn left towards the house. At far side of this bear half right to a stile immediately before the footbridge over the Afon Leri.

2 Cross over and climb up a short distance to join a good, but very narrow and steep path slanting across the hillside above the narrow confine of the attractive waterfall of Craig y Pistyll to your right. Care is required here. The path becomes level and continues, above the Afon Leri to a dam holding back the waters of Llyn Craigypistyll. Follow the path alongside the north-west side of the lake to a stream and a stile immediately beyond. Cross both of these and continue along the path to a track. Go to your right, through the gate and cross a stream. Continue up the track then go right at the next track junction along a bridleway. Follow this and pass the ruins of Bwlchstyllen on your right.

3 The bridleway continues to a gate. Go through this and turn right to walk over the footbridge and follow the track to Llyn Syfydrin. Keep the lake to your right and continue to a track junction. Turn right and walk over the low dam. Follow the narrow tarmac road to a cattle grid. Cross this and continue along the tarmac road to join the minor road at a Y junction. Turn right along the road back to your car.

*T*he water outlet *served the leat, built by John Horridge in 1840. This leat conveyed water from the Afon Leri to Cwmsebon via Llawrcwmbach and Llety-Ifan-Hen, a distance of some 14 miles! The reservoir of Llyn Craigypistyll was dammed in 1880 when John Taylor extended the leat system, thus increasing the overall fall of water.*

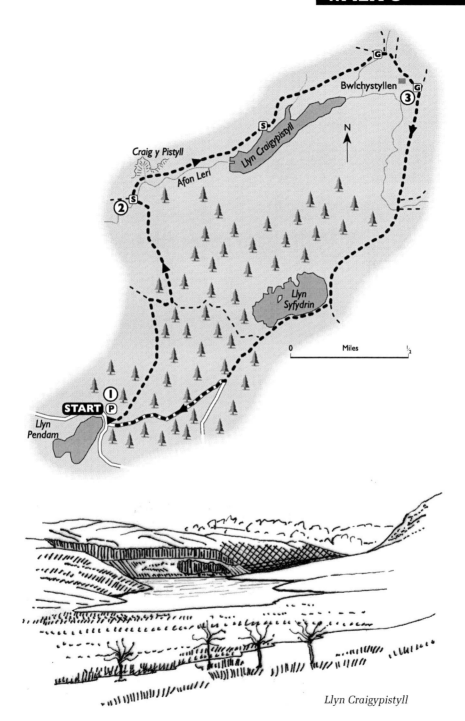

Llyn Craigypistyll

WALK 9
DOLGOCH FALLS

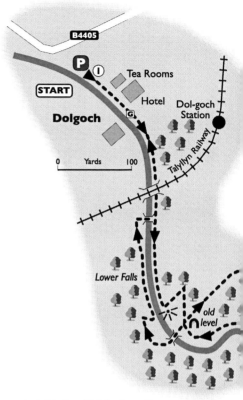

DESCRIPTION A lovely, though quite popular, walk especially in summer which can be very enthralling when the waterfalls are in spate after a period of heavy rainfall. The steeper sections of the path, particularly the steps, can be quite slippery when wet. DO NOT ENTER ANY OF THE ADITS THAT YOU PASS DURING THE WALK. 1½ miles, but allow an hour to admire the falls or it can take all day if having a picnic! There are four bridges each having a poem attached to them. These poems were written by children from the Primary School at Bryncrug.

START The Car Park for Dolgoch Falls on the B4405. There is a parking charge (£1 for 4 hours or £2 all day, May 2007).

DIRECTIONS From Tywyn take the A493 Dolgellau road as far as Bryncrug. Turn right here on to the B4405 signed Talyllyn. The prominent car park close to the Dolgoch Hotel is seen on your right before reaching Abergynolwyn.

I From the car park go up the narrow tarmac road passing to the right of the Dolgoch Falls Hotel. Go through the substantial metal gate ahead and keep following the tarmac track ignoring the sign to Dolgoch Station on your left. Keeping the stream on your right go under the railway bridge and ignore the footbridge on your right. Continue slightly uphill to the viewing area for the lower falls. There is an adit here that leads into the base of a shaft. Return a few metres to the information board and go steeply up steps ignoring the track that continues beyond the metal gate to Dolgoch Station. Keep on this rough track to a junction. Go right to overlook the falls. There is a fenced-off deep shaft to your left. Just before the foot bridge turn sharp left and follow the fence to the corner and bear slightly left away from it to pass a locked gate on your left. Continue uphill through a lovely sessile oak wood on a well marked path. This path meets a fence on your left and a short section of wooden walkway. Easy walking with a protective fence on your right leads to a path junction. Instead of going down the steps to your right continue straight ahead high above the gorge to a bridge over the stream (**Pont 4 – Pont Uchaf**). There is a fine picnic site here complete with tables, benches and shelter!

> 'Cross to the clearing over the narrow gorge
> Reach a meadow above the falls
> the sound of quiet whispers
> Rest, watch and listen to the murmur,
> the tales of the stream
> Mysterious Dolgoch'

2 Return to the steps – now on your left. Go steeply down these and follow the zig-zag path down to stream level. There are good views of the upper falls from this path. Two adits are seen to your right – the last just before the bridge with two names. Pont yr Ogof is one and Pont y Bwa which I think is far more apt – the curved bridge. This is **Pont 3**.

16

'Pass the cave, dangling over a cauldron –
a blue basin rock clinging to the cliff.
Dangling iron hanging over a precipice
oak and steel over water'

Keep following the path with the stream to your left past another picnic area. Another adit is passed with two shelters beyond to your right. Continue to the fenced-off shaft and bridge over the top of the lower falls. This is **Pont 2** – Pont y Pistyll Arian.

'Footbridge over falls
gurgling along the green grey rocks
sliding, zigzagging
See the white fountain – a silver riband
swallowed by a whale of water roaring
    falls'

Cross the bridge, go up steps and continue ahead passing a 'no entry' sign on your left and descend a zig-zag path down to stream level by the lower falls where there is a great view of these. Follow the level path downstream to **Pont 1** – Pont Mur Mwswgl.

'Amber iron flowing from the green moss
Damp gorge split by smooth water
The woodland welcomes
under the large arched viaduct
Follow the track ahead'

Cross the bridge and retrace your steps back to the car park.

Dolgoch Falls were bequeathed to the public through the generosity of a Tywyn chemist – R J Roberts – at the turn of the 20th century. Many improvements were made to the area in 2003 by the Bryncrug Community Council with help from the Snowdonia National Park Authority. The viaduct you walk underneath near the start that carries the Talyllyn Railway was built at a cost of £3000 in 1866.

The gorge is a veritable fern garden. The damp atmosphere from the spray of the waterfalls ensures that there are many varieties perfectly at home here including the scarce Wilson's filmy fern. There are also ten species of liverwort which in times past were believed to cure people of liver disease!

old level

picnic

old level

old level

Upper Falls

picnic

②

Dolgoch Falls

17

WALK 10

CASCADES TRAIL

DESCRIPTION An all-ability trail passing alongside the infant and pretty Afon Hafren (River Severn). The trail ends at a platform with picnic tables and a great view of the many cascades. ½ mile, 30 minutes.

START From the Rhyd-y-Benwch car park. There are toilets and an information board here.

DIRECTIONS From the centre of Llanidloes turn down Short Bridge Street which is opposite the ancient Market Hall. Drive over the bridge spanning the Afon Hafren (River Severn) and turn left. Follow the road and ignoring all turnings continue through Glan-y-Nant to a junction and sharp right hand bend. Go right round the bend – signed 'Hafren 4 miles'. Drive through Old Hall and continue to the Rhyd-y-Benwch car park on your left. From Machynlleth this is easily reached – though longer – by following the mountain road to Staylittle and turning right following the Forestry Commission signs to Hafren Forest and the car park.

To the right of the information board in the car park a marker post indicates the start of all the walks. Follow a gentle downhill, shady and zigzag tarmac path to the River Severn. An obvious boardwalk is followed to its end where there is a fine balcony overlooking the cascades. This is a great spot for a picnic. Either return the same way or follow the tarmac path through the wood with red ringed marker posts to the car park.

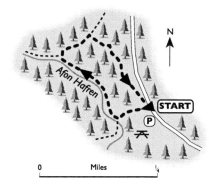

Red Kite

18

WALK 11
'SEVERN-BREAK-ITS-NECK' WATERFALL

DESCRIPTION A lovely walk through fine meadows with the River Severn never very far away. Mature forest gives way to an open area where the Severn plunges into a narrow defile. 1½ miles, 1 hour.

START From the Rhyd y Benwch car park (see **Walk 10**).

1 From the car park follow **Walk 10** to the river. Turn left along a path signed to 'Break-its-Neck Walk' – orange ringed marker posts. Continue by the river edge to a footbridge over the river to your right. Do not cross this but turn left to walk up the steps. At the top follow the right edge of the meadow all the way around passing a group of picnic tables on the way. Follow a boardwalk which ends when you enter a conifer plantation. The path descends to almost reach the river edge. Keep following this path to reach a forest track and turn left. Continue along the track to a gate. Pass through this to a right

turn after 200 yards where sign indicates you have reached 'Severn-Break-its-Neck'. There is fine view of the fall from the footbridge spanning the river.

2 Cross over and walk up to another forest track. Turn right and continue ignoring two right turns. Walk up a short gradual rise to where the track levels and then descends gradually to a Y junction. Take the right arm and walk down and around several bends to the next Y junction. Again take the right arm and continue to a footbridge on your right. Cross this to join the path of your outward journey and either return to the car park OR follow either **Walk 10** to the cascades or continue further to the Blaen Hafren Falls.

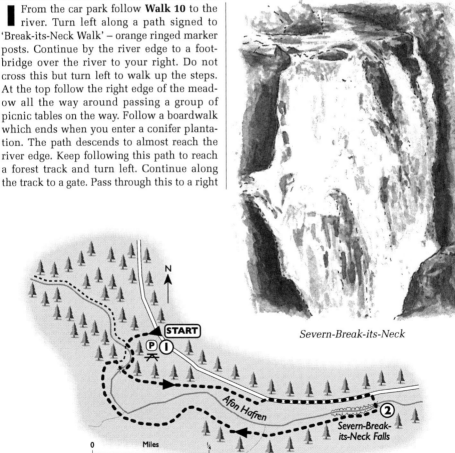

Severn-Break-its-Neck

WALK 12
BLAEN HAFREN FALLS

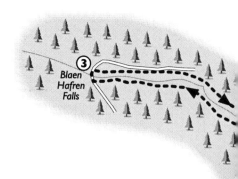

DESCRIPTION A lovely walk following the River Severn with many cascades and a fine waterfall at the farthest point. 3 miles, 1½ hours.
START From the Rhyd y Bengwm car park. There are toilets and an information board here.
DIRECTIONS From the centre of Llanidloes turn down Short Bridge Street which is opposite the ancient Market Hall. Drive over the bridge spanning the Afon Hafren (River Severn) and turn left. Follow the road and ignoring all turnings continue through Glan-y-Nant to a junction and sharp right hand bend. Go right round the bend – signed Hafren 4 miles. Drive through Old Hall and continue to the Rhyd-y-Benwch car park on your left. From Machynlleth this is easily reached – though longer – by following the mountain road to Staylittle and turning right following the Forestry Commission signs to Hafren Forest and the car park.

I To the right of the information board in the car park a marker post indicates the start of all the walks. Follow a gentle downhill, shady and zigzag tarmac path to the River Severn. An obvious boardwalk is followed to its end where there is a fine balcony overlooking the cascades. This is a great spot for a picnic.

2 From the cascades follow blue ringed marker posts to a junction with a track. Turn left and follow the track alongside the river to a right hand bend. Go around this and, still following the Severn on your left, continue to a footbridge. Cross this and turn right at the far side and follow the path with the river now on your right. Keep walking to another footbridge over the river next to a concrete sluice and hut. Cross this. A junction with a track is quickly reached. Turn left along this and bear right uphill following blue ringed marker posts. Keep following the track until a barrier gate is reached. Walk around this on the left and up to a track just beyond. Turn right and ignore – for now – the path going off to your right. Continue along the track to Blaen Hafren Falls.

Blaen Hafren

Blaen Hafren Falls

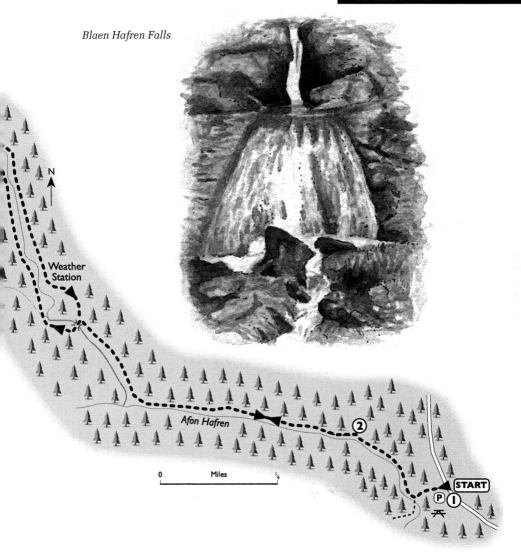

3 Retrace your steps a few yards and take the path going down on your left – blue ringed marker post a few yards down – and follow it until you reach a junction with a track. Bear left here – another blue ringed marker post ahead – until the track goes sharply right close to a hut and railings. Continue until you reach the footbridge over the river by the concrete sluice and hut passed on your outward journey. Retrace your steps back to the car park.

PISTYLL CAIN & RHAEADR MAWDDACH

DESCRIPTION This is a lovely, though quite popular walk with two very fine waterfalls, especially after heavy rain. The walk is entirely on tracks or made up paths DO NOT ENTER ANY OF THE ADITS THAT YOU PASS DURING THE WALK. 2 miles, allow an 1½ hours to admire the falls.

START At the forest picnic site – Tyddyn Glwyadys – which is located almost at the end of the tarmac road.

DIRECTIONS From Dolgellau follow the A470 towards Betws y Coed. Go through the village of Ganllwyd to the far end, where, close to the speed de-restriction signs, turn right. Cross the bridge over the river and bear right. Follow the minor road to the picnic site.

1 Walk back to the road from the picnic site. Turn right and follow the tarmac road to its end and continue along a rough track passing through a gate ahead signed to Ferndale. Pass to the left of the barrier – partly flooded adit here – and continue along the track above the holiday cottages on your right. Keep walking along the track above the tumbling Afon Mawddach with many small cascades to a bridge which spans the tributary river the Afon Cain. Cross the bridge.

2 Immediately beyond the bridge a well worn but very narrow and slippery path – TAKE CARE – allows you to observe the Pistyll Cain at close quarters. Returning to the track continue left to a track junction. Bear right here passing ruins of the old gold mine of Gwynfynnyd to your left. *Gold was found here in 1864.* To see the Rhaeadr Mawddach in full glory it is possible reach the waters edge by a small path that goes through the ruins and over a pipe to the riverside. Again CARE is needed on the often slippery rock. Return to the track junction. Turn right, up

Rhaeadr Mawddach

slope, and continue to a bridge spanning the Afon Mawddach. There are the remains of an old mill race here which must have carried a fair quantity of water at one stage.

3 Cross the bridge and walk up to a track junction. Go right down the track and continue along to another junction and go straight ahead. Orange and blue markers indicate the way. Ignore the first turning on your right and continue to the next where there is a blue marker indicating the way. Turn right and cross the footbridge spanning the Afon Mawddach and follow the path back to the car park and picnic site.

*T**he difference** in the Welsh names for waterfalls – Pistyll and Rhaeadr – is that Pistyll relates to a narrow or funnel type of fall, whilst Rhaeadr indicates a much wider spread of water.*

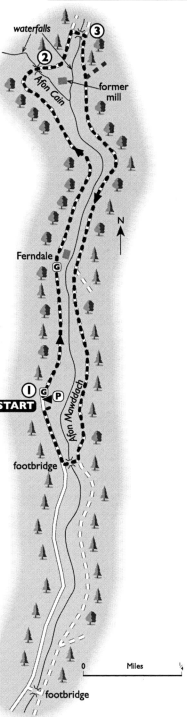

Pistyll Cain

RHAEADR DU

DESCRIPTION These very fine waterfalls are aptly named and are set in lovely woodland. It is not unusual to see herons here.

START At the National Trust car park in Ganllwyd

DIRECTIONS From Dolgellau take the A470 towards Betws y Coed and continue to the village of Ganllwyd. The car park – signed – is on your right just after entering the village. There is an information board and toilet facilities here.

1 From the car park cross the road and turn left to the village hall. Turn right here and go through a gate alongside the hall. Walk up the narrow road with the lovely Afon Gamlan to your left. Bear left at the 'Y' junction for a hundred yards where you can go to your left to the river side. Follow this delightful stretch to where the path becomes rougher and more slippery just before a footbridge.

2 Cross this and turn right along a better defined path although somewhat rough,

to the lower falls. From here a steeper continuation continues to the even more impressive upper falls. Continue beyond these falls on the rough path to a marker post. Go straight ahead to a fence and wall with a stile. Go over this and walk upstream for 100 yards to admire lower but still quite fine waterfalls. Return to the marker post. Turn right here and go gently uphill to a marker post close to the wall. Keep following this path with the wall to your right until you reach another marker post close to a tiny steam. There is a stile on the right here.

3 Ignore this and cross the stream via a tiny footbridge and continue to a kissing gate. Go through this and 100 yards further, a marker post is reached. Turn left here and walk downhill on a wide, well marked path with a wall and stream on your right. Continue downhill to a stunted finger post. Go through the gate ahead and walk down to the wall on your right. This is followed to a stile left of a gate. Cross this and continue down to a gap in the wall to the left of a tiny slate roofed outhouse. Keeping the wall to your right go down to a gate and the main road. Turn left back to your car.

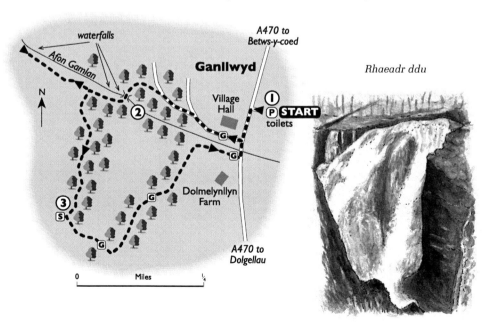

Rhaeadr ddu

24

WALK 15

BRITHDIR TORRENT WALK

DESCRIPTION This is a pretty walk through woodland, initially going down one side of the tumbling Afon Clywedog and back along the other. The stream is at its best after heavy rainfall! 2½ miles, 1½ hours.

START At a large lay-by on the left hand side of the B4416, just before the school in Brithdir.

DIRECTIONS Take the A470 east from Dolgellau towards Machynlleth. After about 2 miles turn LEFT (east) along the B4416 towards Brithdir. After crossing the narrow bridge over the river, park in the first lay-by on the left side, a distance of ½ mile from the main A470 road.

1 Walk to the wooden gate by the lay-by. Go through and follow the path between fences. Continue along the path, with the falls to your left. *The road to your right is thought to be the line of an old Roman road leading to, and beyond, a Roman fortlet at Brithdir about 1 mile to the east. You are now walking on what was the original route of the Torrent walk, and which has been recently*

restored. You pass through two gates and walk behind some beautifully constructed wooden barriers before reaching the road, where you turn left.

2 Cross the briodge and turn left into the Torrent Walk. For some way ahead the path remains close to and on about the same level as the river (ignore the path going up the 12 steps to the right) but it gradually climbs, eventually leaving the river well below. However, the ascent is never steep, and there are short flights of steps in places

to assist the climb. *The beauty of the gorge, and the continually varying views of the Clywedog tumbling over and around the rocks and boulders in its path, make this a walk to be taken slowly. There is a seat, about two thirds of the way up the path, provided by the North Wales Wildlife Trust in memory of Mary Richards, a well known local botanist who died in 1977. At the top of the ravine cross the footbridge over the river (constructed about 1970 to replace Thomas Payne's original crossing) and go out through the gate ahead to the road. Turn left along the road to return to the lay-by just 100 yards ahead.*

*T*he 'Torrent Walk' was designed and engineered by Thomas Payne who also designed the Cob – a raised embankment over the estuary at Porthmadog. He died in 1834 aged 73. There is a memorial plaque to him in St Mark's church. The church is well worth a visit. It is a Grade I listed building, one of only a few in Wales. It has been taken over by the Friends of Friendless Churches, a voluntary organisation formed in 1957 by Ivor Bulmer-Thomas to save churches and chapels of historic and architectural interest which are threatened by demolition or conversion. The church was built between 1885 and 1895 to the designs of Henry Wilson and is one of only a few Art Nouveau churches in Wales. The choir stalls are made from Spanish chestnut and are superbly carved. The architects dream was that 'the church should appear as if it had sprung out of the soil'.

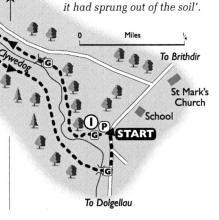

25

LLYN MORWYNION & RHAEADR-Y-CWM

DESCRIPTION This fine and scenic walk stats at the high point. It initially visits the lovely Llyn Morwynion having two legends associated with it, before descending into the quiet, wooded Cwm Cynfal. Finally a climb up the steep hill gives superb views of the dramatic Rhaeadr-y-Cwm. 6 miles, 4 hours.

START At a parking area just off the B4407 close to Llyn Dubach, 2½ miles east of Ffestiniog

DIRECTIONS From Blaenau Ffestiniog follow the A470 to Ffestiniog. Immediately beyond the railway bridge turn left on to the B4391. Some 2½ miles further, turn left at Pont yr Afon Gam by the old petrol station – now a great café with excellent food – on to the B4407. The parking area is found on your left after a ¼ mile.

I Walk along the track on the left side of Llyn Dubach towards the conspicuous white post. Cross the dilapidated stile to the right of the post and continue with the fence to your left. The fence curves leftwards and a stile is soon reached. Cross this and walk down to Llyn Morwynion. Continue around the lake to the dam. The first part of this section can be extremely boggy!

2 Cross the dam and follow the path over an outflow to the very end of the lake. Keep walking straight ahead to a rusting metal gate. Go through this and bear left downhill on a path to a ruin. Continue ahead following a rusting pipe for 100 yards before bearing left and down to a metal gate in the wall on your left. Go through the gate and walk half right to a wall corner and a faint path. The wall turns right so continue ahead away from the wall towards a pole for a short distance then bear half left across boggy ground to a footpath sign and stile. Go over this to join the B4391.

3 Turn right and in 30 yards turn left through a gate and down a track. Continue following this track to a wall corner and pole. There is a railway sleeper on your right here. Turn right to step over this and continue ahead – on a vague track. Continue through a wall to reach a path following the wall on your right. Follow this to a stile. Go over this and follow the fence on your right for 100 yards and then bear half left across the field to a gate in a wall. Go through the gate and follow the fence on your right down to where it ends and an obvious turn on to a farm track. Continue on this track to the farm where the track bears right and continue down to a cross cattle grid. A narrow tarmac road is reached shortly after.

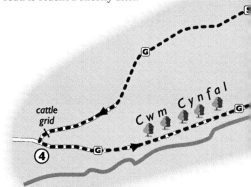

4 Turn left along this road where you will pass the ruin of an old chapel – *Capel y Babell, which was built in 1861.* Walk along the pretty and wooded Cwm Cynfal with the Afon Cynfal not far below. Ignore all turnings (if you cross the river you have gone wrong) and go through three gates to reach Cwm Farm. PLEASE DO NOT walk through the yard.

5 Just before the gate leading into it there is a gate (with a waymark) on your left. Go through this and turn right immediately. Continue straight ahead through a gap in the wall beyond and continue to a ladder stile. Cross this and turn immediately left for the steep ascent of the hillside on a well marked path. At the top of the rise there are spectacular views of this fine and dramatic waterfall.

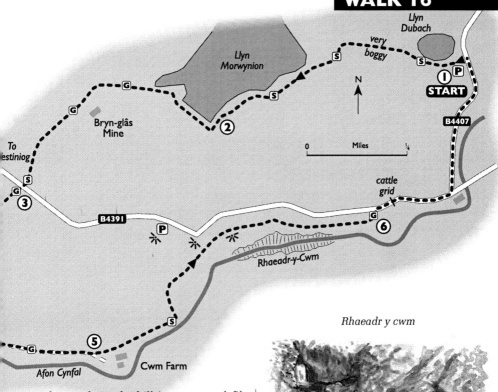

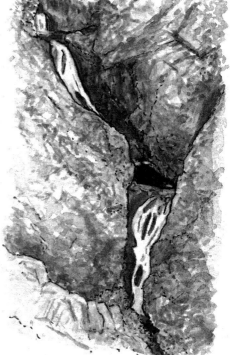

Rhaeadr y cwm

It plunges down the hill in a narrow defile into the valley in six spectacular leaps. The path now bears right. Walking is easier with the path running parallel to the road. Some sections are a little boggy. Continue to the second gate on your left.

6 Go through this onto the road – TAKE CARE – and turn right. Follow the road, walk over a cattle grid and continue to Pont-yr-Afon Gam – *which was, until quite recently Wales' highest petrol station but now serves delicious home made cakes and other snacks.* Turn left here along the B4407 and return to your car.

Llyn Morwynion *is a beautiful gem. The Lake of Maidens refers to Blodeuedd and her Maidens of Ardudwy who supposedly drowned here when fleeing from Gwydion. Another version says that the women had become attracted to the Men of Ardudwy having been carried off by them. When the Men of Clwyd came to reclaim them they threw themselves into the lake in despair!*

WALK 17

RHAEADR CYNFAL

DESCRIPTION Once across farmland a splendid waterfall is visited and continues through some fine woodland in a steep sided valley. The return walk from the road at Pont Tal-y-bont is steadily uphill giving good views over towards Ffestiniog and the Moelwyns. 2½ miles, 2 hours.

START Close to the church in Ffestiniog.

DIRECTIONS From Blaenau Ffestiniog continue along the A470 towards Ffestiniog. At the sharp left hand bend turn right and a few yards further on there is parking below the church close to the Pengwern Arms. From Dolgellau follow the A470 to Ffestiniog. Instead of going around the sharp right hand bend continue for 200 yards to the church and parking area.

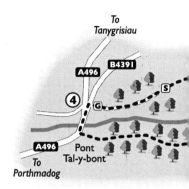

1 Walk to your right along the road. A metal gate on your left is soon reached. Pass through this – sign to Rhaeadr Cynfal Falls. Continue ahead then turn left through a swing gate and walk across and down the field to a metal gate. Pass through this and go over a small bridge and follow the path to another metal gate. Go through this and walk with a wall to your left and pass through a wooden gate. Turn right and continue to two metal gates. Go through the left hand of two and follow the sign to Cynfal on the obvious path going gently downhill keeping the wall to your left to a gate. Go through this.

2 The right hand of the fork of paths takes you to a viewpoint over the falls. The water tumbles into a dark and sombre fissure. *Downstream there is a high, pulpit shaped block. This is known as Huw Lloyd's Pulpit. He lived in Cynfal Fawr a little to the south and in the 17thC came here to preach, recite poetry as well as trying to raise the Devil!! Apparently the Devil was a non-swimmer. Huw's activities were recorded by Thomas Love Peacock (1785 – 1866) in his novel 'Headlong Hall'.* Return to the path and descend steps to a bridge with a gate. Cross the bridge and climb up steps on the far side.

3 Go through the gate at the top of the steps and continue ahead following the path which veers away from the waterfall to a metal gate. Go through this and continue to another gate. Go through this and follow the path with a fence to your right and go through a gate. Walk down to another. Go through this and follow the path down the hill as it weaves through trees and continue down through a gate and to arrive at a road by the Pont Tal-y-bont.

4 Turn right over the bridge and right again immediately after the bridge over a way-marked stile. Follow the track. Where the track forks follow the left hand one and continue up to a stile. Go over this and continue straight ahead keeping a broken wall to your left. Go through a gap in the wall and keeping the wall to your right now walk towards a pylon. When the path forks go right through another gap in the wall and the pylon to your right. *There is a grand view of the Moelwyns from here. To your right an obelisk is seen. This is a memorial to William Charles IVth, Baron Newborough who died on the 19th July 1916 aged 42.* Go through a gate and on through another to reach a road, the B4391. Turn right and continue along the path to your car in the village.

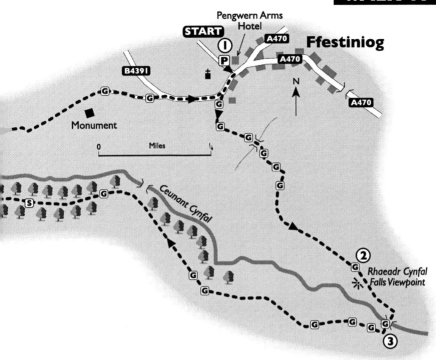

Huw Lloyd was, what we might consider today, a white wizard! People such as Huw were fairly common in the 17thC, all claiming to be the seventh son of a seventh son. Some wizards did sell their souls to the Devil by drinking holy water then spitting it out immediately, which put them in contact with Devil. Although well educated he found that he could make a jolly good income from the mostly illiterate local population. One farmer, however, did not take Huw's sermons from his pulpit in the gorge seriously and shouted obscenities. True to from Huw cursed the man who, a few days later, found that his cattle were dying. Distraugt, the farmer begged Huw to forgive him. He was but, obviously, at a cost.

RHAEADR DDU

DESCRIPTION There are three such named waterfalls in Wales. Quiet lanes, woodland and a fine waterfall are visited on this gentle walk through the beautiful Ceunant Llenyrch, a National Nature Reserve. 3½ miles, 2½ hours.

START At the car park in Gellilydan.

DIRECTIONS From Blaenau Ffestiniog continue along the A470 towards Ffestiniog. Turn sharp left and keep on the main road to a 'T' junction. Turn right onto the A487 and continue downhill for a short distance until a sign for Gellilydan indicates where you turn left into the village. At the 'Y' junction turn right. The car park is 200 yards further on your left. From Dolgellau follow the A470. By-pass Trawsfynnyd and continue to where the A470 turns right. Do not turn here but continue towards Porthmadog on the A487 to where the sign for Gellilydan indicates a left turn into the village. Continue as above to the car park.

Rejoin the road and turn right. Turn right again by the Pen-y-bont stores. Walk past the modern looking Bryn Arms pub along this lovely quiet lane with good views. When the lane turns to the right at Bryntirion walk to the left along a track and on through a gateway.

2 The track soon splits. Go to your right and continue passing through a gate. Ignore the track going off to your left and continue through another gate and soon go over a bridge above an enormous pipe. *This pipe carries water to the Maentwrog Hydro Electric Power Station. This has a capacity of 24,000 KW and is located some 1½ miles north of here. The water comes from Llyn Trawsfynnyd, a man-made feature dating from 1926. In 1965 the Llyn*

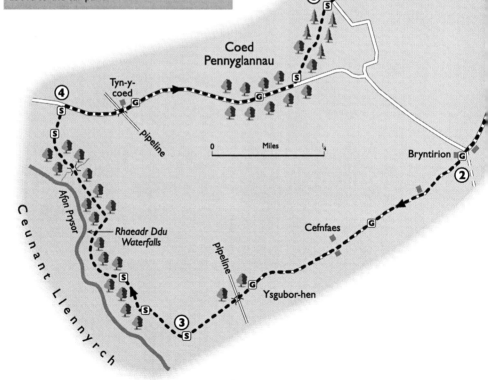

Tyn-y-coed

Coed Pennyglannau

Rhaeadr Ddu Waterfalls

Afon Prysor

Ceunant Llennyrch

Bryntirion

Cefnfaes

Ysgubor-hen

pipeline

Miles

N

provided *32 million gallons of cooling water for the now defunct Nuclear Power Station.* Continue straight ahead through a gateway and along the right hand side of a field.

3 A stile is reached. Cross over this and walk half right across the field to another stile. Cross this and enter forestry following the path around to the right. The path descends towards a stream. Cross this and a stile and continue downhill to where a track crosses. Just after passing through a

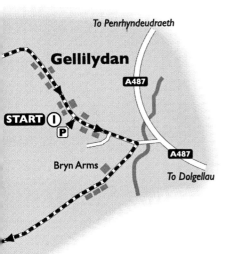

To Penrhyndeudraeth

Gellilydan

A487

START (1) (P)

Bryn Arms

A487

To Dolgellau

gap in the wall a path branches off to the left from where the upper falls can be explored, BEWARE, the path is very slippery. Continue along the track through the wood to meet another track at a 'T' junction. *There is a fine view of the falls to your left.* It is possible to obtain a much better view of the falls by descending a wide path with steps that descends to the stream. DO NOT ENTER the stream as SUDDEN flash flooding can occur, especially when water is released from Llyn Trawsfynnyd. Turn right at the 'T' junction and continue along the obvious path. Cross a footbridge and follow the track as it gently climbs the side of the gorge. The path eventually turns sharply to your right and ascends to a gate. Go through this and continue to another gate.

4 Go through the gate, turn right and walk along the lane which again crosses the pipeline. Go through a gate and continue passing through another to reach yet another one and a stile on your left. Go over the stile and follow the path into the gloom of the trees. You emerge at a stile. Go over this and cross the lane.

5 Go through a small metal gate and continue ahead. Walk to the right of the buildings to reach a ladder stile. Cross this and follow the path to your left through trees. Go through a gate next to a cottage and continue to join the road. Turn right and back to your car.

Rhaeadr Cynfal

31

WALK 19
CWM NANTCOL

DESCRIPTION This is a gentle and beautiful valley walk through rugged terrain with spectacular views of the Rhinog Mountains. Towards the end of the walk there is a pretty, though small, waterfall. This is a great place for a picnic and/or a swim. 2½ miles, 1½ hours.

START From a large pull in on the left hand side of the road opposite a telephone and post box at Capel Nantcol.

DIRECTIONS From Barmouth follow the A496 to Llanbedr. Immediately beyond the Victoria Inn turn right signed to Cwm Nantcol and Cwm Bychan. (If coming from Harlech turn left just before the Victoria Inn). Turn right a mile or so up this road – signed Cwm Nantcol and cross the Afon Cwmnantcol. Take the first turning left and continue to the pull in on the left hand side of the narrow road where there is ample room for a number of cars.

a gap through a wall. Walk gradually up past a way marker. At the next way marker, just before a small rocky bluff, bear right across a tiny stream to the next way marker. A better path is now followed up to yet another marker. Bear right passing a slab of rock on tour right and drop down to a boggy area. At the far side of this step up through a wall with a way marker and follow the path through a gap in the wall and continue to a gate. Go through this and follow the path to the narrow tarmac road.

2 Turn right and cross Pont Cerrig. Immediately beyond the bridge climb over the ladder stileon your right. A faint path is followed through sedges to a clapper bridge. Cross this and follow an even fainter path, keeping the stream on your right, to a metal 'bed-head' gate! Go through this where a clearer path continues and goes over two footbridges. After the second bridge a ladder stile is seen ahead some 300 yards distant. Head towards this. At first along a faint path then through a boggy area to reach the stile. Cross over and keeping to the high ground (there is a small waterfall on your right just after the stile) bear right to a sycamore tree by a low wall. Turn right here and follow a vague path keeping the wall to your left to where the path crosses the wall. Follow the faint

1 From the parking area go through an ancient metal gate and follow the signed path down to reach another ancient gate very quickly. Go through this and turn right alongside a wall. At the next gate in the wall on your right – way marker – turn left and continue ahead to reach a fence by the Afon Cwmnantcol. Turn right here keeping the fence to your left and continue to a footbridge over the river. Cross this and turn right. Follow the well marked path keeping a drainage ditch to your right and continue to a ladder stile. Cross over this and continue past a ruin to some stone steps leading up to

path along the edge of a very boggy area to your left to where a grassy nook is reached by the pretty, though small, waterfall. *This is great place for a picnic and/or a swim!* Continue to the ladder stile. Cross this and walk half left up to some farm buildings. Pass these on your left and continue on a good path keeping the wall to your left to a gate with a way marker. Do not go through the gate but the follow the way markers to the next ladder stile. Go over this and keeping close to the wall follow the path to join your outward journey and a short walk back to your car.

WALK 20

PISTYLL GWYN

DESCRIPTION Although basically a there and back walk the waterfall is a magnificent one in a hidden upland valley. There is a novel stream crossing half way! For the adventurous there is a strenuous option. This follows a very steep path up the side of the waterfall to view the top falls which are hidden from below. GREAT CARE is required towards the top as the path is narrow and weaves through small rocky bluffs. 2½ miles, 1½ hours if going to the base of the fall OR 3 miles, 2½ hours for the option. Combined with **Walk 23** this makes a fine day out in the upper Dyfi Valley.

START From the telephone box in Llanymawddwy.

DIRECTIONS As for **Walk 23** but park in the large pull in by the telephone box in Llanymawddwy village.

to the far side. Go left to a stile. Go over this and then walk up half right to reach a field. Turn left at a vague grassy track and follow this to a ladder stile. Cross this and follow the green track to a stream. Looking up to your right here you can see a small waterfall. Cross the steam. The path climbs easily and then levels and continues to the base of the fall. There is a stone built shelter hereabouts.

2 Return to the stream crossing by the small waterfall and bear right to the Afon Pumryd. On the far side is a ladder stile. Stepping stones, close to a wire fence in the stream, aid the crossing. Climb over the stile and walk up to a narrow path. Turn left along this to reach the track of your outward walk and return to your car.

Optional variation – For the adventurous it is possible to climb up a narrow path to the top falls hidden from below. Return along the path a short distance to a prominent large rock on your left and walk up left to join a narrow path slanting up and left. A grassy, narrow rake can be seen crossing the hillside. This path follows that,

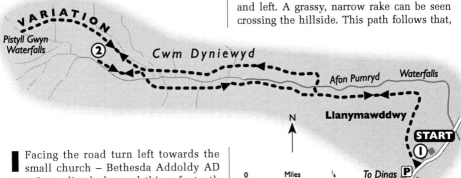

I Facing the road turn left towards the small church – Bethesda Addoldy AD 1884. Immediately beyond this a footpath indicates a turn right. Follow this path up to a ladder stile. Cross this to join a concrete and very steep track - thankfully short lived – to where it levels. Continue to a building to where the track turns 90 degrees to the left. Keep walking alongside a small plantation and fence on your right to where these end and the first view of Pistyll Gwyn is seen ahead. Continue along the track to where it ends. Drop down half right to where there is a metal pole spanning the stream – *Afon Pumryd (the stream of five fords)*. Using this and a large convenient flat rock step across

getting steeper as height is gained. GREAT CARE is required towards the top as the path weaves between small rocky bluffs. Eventually the path reaches a fantastic tiny belvedere of flat grass at the top of the main falls from which there are remarkable views down the valley and top falls. Return the same way to join point **2** above at the stream crossing.

WALK 21

ARTHOG FALLS & THE CREGENNAN LAKES

DESCRIPTION This is an extremely varied and scenic walk. It initially follows the embankment of Afon Arthog before climbing alongside some very pretty waterfalls and cascades. Having left these behind the walk continues across grazing land, with increasingly good views of the Mawddach estuary and Barmouth, before walking up a short section of road to the Cregennan Lakes. After visiting these the walk returns via grazing land and back down alongside the waterfalls. 4 miles, 3 hours

START At the Snowdonia National Park, Arthog, car park.

DIRECTIONS From Dolgellau take the A493 towards Tywyn. Drive through Penmaenpool and continue to Arthog. Go past St Catherine's church on your right until a prominent green corrugated hut is seen at the junction with a side road. Turn right down here – signed to Min-y-Don – to the car park.

I Leave the car park and turn right after passing through the gate. Continue a short distance to a way marker and ladder stile on your left. Climb over this and follow the embankment above the Afon Arthog and then along to the A493 by the side of St. Catherine's church. Go through a kissing gate onto the road and turn left a very short distance to where there is a small gate on your right opposite the church. Walk up the steps to an old gateway. Pass through this and in 25m turn right onto a smaller path. Follow this up passing several small cascades and larger falls and around a sharp right hand bend. Continue along the easier graded path along the top of the narrow gorge. Cross over a ladder stile and more falls are encountered before crossing another ladder stile to reach a green track and a very fine 'clapper bridge' over the Afon Arthog.

2 Cross this and follow a grassy path up to join a farm track. Turn left up this and continue through a gate. Carry straight on up to another. Go through this. Keep close to the wall on your left and continue to a marker post by a ruined building on your left. Continue to where the wall turns 90 degrees to the left and follow a farm track between walls for 50 yards. Turn right through the gap here – there is a marker post – and walk across the field to the prominent ladder stile. Climb over this and follow the grassy path past a marker post. Continue through the bouldery continuation of the path to a gate in the wall ahead. Go through this and follow marker posts to a ladder stile on your left which is climbed over to follow more marker posts down through a small gap in the wall. Go left immediately through another gap and follow the wall on your right down to the narrow tarmac road.

3 Turn right up this and continue uphill past Cefn-hir-isaf. Go through a gate just beyond and continue steeply to where the road levels and a footpath sign on your left. Turn left along this path across to a ladder stile over a wall. Cross this and follow the level path ahead to a marker post. Turn right and follow a less well defined and boggy path to a marker post. Drop down to the lake shore and continue on the path by the shore to a ladder stile over a fence. Cross this and almost immediately cross a smaller stile. Turn left. Continue to a marker post by the shore of the second of the Cregennan Lakes. Turn right and follow the path by the shore to a boathouse. This has a ladder stile next to it. Cross this and continue along the path to where it veers away from the lake at a fence. Keep walking ahead to join a narrow tarmac road and a marker post. Turn right along the road and pass a standing stone 50 yards up on your right. Keep going and pass Ffridd Boedal on your left, where fishing permits may be obtained, to a gate. Go through this and around a sharp left hand hairpin bend. Just past a small conifer plantation there is a footpath sign on your left.

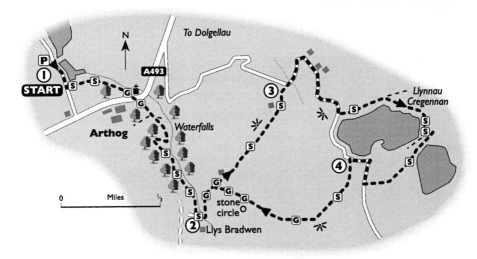

4 Turn left here along the wide grassy path to a fine, stone step, stile. Climb over this and follow the path alongside the wall on your right to where the path veers away to the left at some yellow arrows painted on the wall. Keep walking along this path and then drop down to a Llwybr Cyhoeddus sign and gate. Go through the gate and keeping the wall to your left continue to another footpath sign. Turn right here and keeping the wall to your left continue to another gate. Go through this. Just before going through the field on your left has a fine stone circle. Continue keeping the wall on your left to another gate. Go through this. A short distance ahead you join a farm track. Bearing left along this you reach a gate where you join your outward walk. Retrace your steps back to the clapper bridge and down alongside the falls to your car.

Cregennan Lakes

WALK 22

HIRGWM WATERFALLS

DESCRIPTION The falls are close to the start this is a pretty, though short walk in the 'gold mining belt' of mid-Wales. There are some good views of the Mawddach estuary and Cadair Idris. The Afon Hirgwm is spectacular after heavy rainfall. 2 miles, 1½ hours.

START At a large pull in 440 yards beyond the phone box in Llechfraith.

DIRECTIONS From Dolgellau follow the A496 towards Barmouth to Bontddu. At the Bontddu Hall Hotel turn right and drive up the very steep road. Pass several houses and a phone box on your right at a junction. Bear left over Pont Hirgwm. Continue along the road to a gate. Go through this – PLEASE CLOSE – and continue to a steep right hand hairpin bend. There is a large pull in on your left before going around it for several cars.

I Walk back down the road to the phone box. Continue a few yards to a gate on your left. This is opposite a footpath sign. (A path goes off to your right here and goes back towards the bridge. An awkward rock step is very slippery in wet weather – CARE NEEDED – gives access to view the spectacular waterfalls). Go through the gate and follow the track uphill. *There are good views of Diffwys one of the main Rhinog Mountains from here.* A house – Ty'n y Cornel – is passed on the right and the barn on the left as the track descends slightly. Go through a gate at the end of the barn. Follow the track up and in a short distance a building with a wriggly tin roof is passed on your left. Here turn sharp right to find an adit into the upper reaches of Clogau gold mine. *This locked and barred adit still has a tram line in situ with one of the drams. The St David's lode of Clogau was one of the richest and productive in the area. In 1862 it promoted a Klondyke style gold rush into the area. Gold was first found in 1853 and was worked until the early part of the 20thC.*

2 Return to the gate at the end of the barn by Ty'n y Cornel, turn around and take the left hand track that descends towards some old mine workings. Immediately bear left again taking a path that crosses a stream and head up to a wall where there is a yellow topped post with a stone and concrete stile. Cross this and walk up the rise. Ignore the gate on your left. Keep close to the wall on your left. Bear left at a junction where a path and a wall come in from the right. Continue ahead between two walls. Cross a stream, pass a wooden gate in the wall to your left and bear right immediately after this. Cross a very fine 'clapper bridge' over the Afon Cwm Llechen. Bear left to rejoin the track and walk uphill to a gate and a stile. Go over the stile. Continue up and along the track with a wall to your left. When the track levels out a wooden gate is reached again with a stile. Go over this. Continue up the track and through a stream to reach a locked gate with a stile. Go over the stile to join a tarmac lane. *There is a good view of Cadair Idris brooding high above the Afon Mawddach.*

3 Walk straight ahead passing immediately through a gate and continue quite steeply uphill. Pass a yellow marker and continue to a junction by a roofless barn. Turn left here down a grassy track. This soon turns into a concreted surface and go through a gate with a yellow marker. Continue to a stile over a wall on the left – footpath sign. Go over the stile and bear left and then immediately turn right over another stile and enter woodland. Turn left at a yellow arrow just beyond the stile and walk downhill keeping close to the fence on your left. As the Afon Hirgwm comes into sight bear left and follow the path down. Pass by a metal gate on your left and cross over a stream where there is a yellow marker. Go AHEAD here although it appears to be obvious to go downhill to the right. Keep close to the fence on your left to reach a stile over a wall. Go over the stile and the path trends down to the river again with a fence to your left. Pass an empty reservoir on your right before reaching the road at your car.

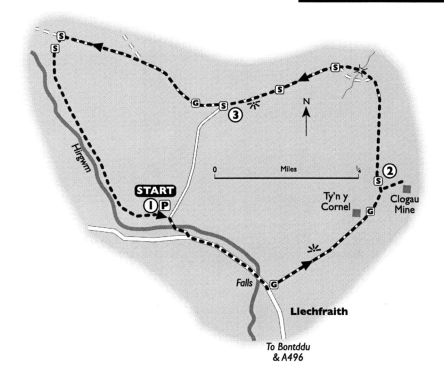

Tyn y Cornel adit

LLAETHNANT WATERFALLS

DESCRIPTION This is a fine but short walk for the adventurous. A magnificent set of falls plunging down the steep valley are reached by faint paths that lead to and away from them. GREAT CARE is required when following the bank of the river as the paths are not easy to find. There are some vertical drops on your left which plunge directly into the turbulent river below. However, these are easily avoided on your right. An old pipe can be followed in places. The Llaethnant is the main tributary that forms the Afon Dyfi. 2 miles, 1½ hours.

START From the acute right hand hairpin bend on the Bwlch y Groes road where there is a gate and a ladder stile.

DIRECTIONS From Machynlleth follow the A458 to the roundabout in Cemmaes Road. At the roundabout turn left onto the A470 towards Dolgellau. Continue across the roundabout in Mallwyd still on the A470, to Dinas Mawddwy. Turn right into the village and at the Llew Goch pub turn right on to the minor road and continue along this through Llanymawddwy to the sharp right hand hairpin bend. There is parking downhill from this bend.

I From the apex of the bend cross the ladder stile and walk along the track to a gate. Do not go through this but pass it to the right – way marker. Continue along the path to another ladder stile. Cross this and continue along the green track to a stream. Up to your right there are some pretty falls. A short distance beyond the track splits. The main track goes uphill. Turn to your left here. Keep the fence and small plantation to your left and continue to a gate where the fence turns to the right. Still keeping

the fence to your left continue to the edge of the river. Intermittent faint paths now lead up the side of the river where GREAT CARE is needed. This section of the walk is very spectacular. A pipe acts as a guide in several places. At the top of the main falls bear to the right of a large rock bluff. Vague paths now continue between smaller bluffs where there are smaller though still attractive falls. Continue to a large flat grassy area by a deep pool and small fall just before the river emerges from a narrow ravine. Bear right here to join the main track. It is worth a short walk up the track to admire the splendid valley with the infant Llaethnant flowing through. Turn around and follow the track down to the track junction of your outward journey and on to your car.

L *lanymawddwy is famous for two giants. Llewellyn Fawr o Fawddwy is buried in the churchyard. It is said that human bones twice the normal size were unearthed here. These were thought to belong to Cawr Mawddwy who threw a rock from the top of Aran Fawddwy leaving indentations where is fingers held it. The rock – Maen y Cawr lies on Ffridd Wenallt – the prominent sharp ridge above the hairpin bend .*

Llamymawddwy is on a drovers road, which are found throughout Wales. They were used to drive cattle and other stock to the markets in England. The drovers then faced a perilous journey home with their pockets full of money and were prey to being robbed. It was also a very spiritual place because the drovers and pilgrims prayed before tackling the pass. They also needed places to rest and at one time there were seven pubs in the village with names linked to droving, such as – Blue Horse, Bull Mawr, Bull Bach and The Goat.

38

WALK 24

CADAIR CATARACTS

DESCRIPTION Although this is a there and back walk it is a grand experience. Not only does the steep path climb alongside the tumbling Nant Cadair, the walk can be continued into the very heart of Cadair Idris at Llyn Cau. This is a magnificent lake with the stupendous Craig Cau beyond. The falls are best appreciated after heavy rainfall when they look like flowing milk. 3 miles, 2 hours.

START At the Snowdonia National Park car park at Minffordd.

DIRECTIONS Take the A487 from Machynlleth towards Dolgellau. Drive through the village of Corris and continue to a road junction. Turn left here, on to the B4405 and, almost immediately, turn right into the car park There is a parking fee payable here.

Leave the car park by the toilet block and pass through a kissing gate. Turn right at the track and follow the avenue of horse chestnut trees to another kissing gate. This is immediately before Ystradlyn, the Countryside Commission for Wales Information Centre. Walk in front of the building and cross a bridge over the Nant Cadair. At the far side turn right and pass through a gate. This is the start of a steep climb with steps, never far from a tumbling stream. Continue to a gate. Pass through this. The gradient lessens here and continues to a junction. This is the end of the waterfall section. However, you have done all the hard work and it seems a pity to turn round and walk back The walking is now much easier to Llyn Cau and is thoroughly recommended. Walk back the same way.

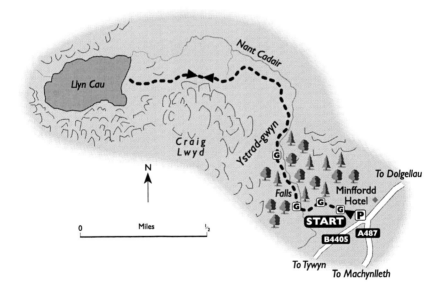

PRONUNCIATION

These basic points should help non-Welsh speakers

Welsh	English equivalent
c	always hard, as in cat
ch	as on the Scottish word loch
dd	as 'th' in then
f	as 'f' in of
ff	as 'ff' in off
g	always hard as in got
ll	no real equivalent. It is like 'th' in then, but with an 'L' sound added to it, giving 'thlan' for the pronunciation of the Welsh 'Llan'.

In Welsh the accent usually falls on the last-but-one syllable of a word.

KEY TO THE MAPS

——— Main road

═══ Minor road

•-► Walk route and direction

Ⓘ Walk instruction

– – – Path

∿ River/stream

Ⓖ Gate

Ⓢ Stile

△ Summit

🌲🌳 Woods

🍺 Pub

Ⓟ Parking

THE COUNTRYSIDE CODE

• Be safe – plan ahead and follow any signs

• Leave gates and property as you find them

• Protect plants and animals, and take your litter home

• Keep dogs under close control

• Consider other people

The CroW Act 2000, implemented throughout Wales in May 2005, introduced new legal rights of access for walkers to designated open country, predominantly mountain, moor, heath or down, plus all registered common land. This access can be subject to restrictions and closure for land management or safety reasons for up to 28 days a year.

Published by
Kittiwake
3 Glantwymyn Village Workshops, Glantwymyn, Machynlleth, Montgomeryshire SY20 8LY

© Text & map research: Des Marshall 2009
© Maps & illustrations: Kittiwake 2009
Drawings by Morag Perrott (except pages 9 & 15).

Cover photos: *Main* – Rhaeadr Mawddach.
Inset – Pistll Gwyn. Both by Des Marshall.

Care has been taken to be accurate.
However neither the author nor the publisher can accept responsibility for any errors which may appear, or their consequences. If you are in any doubt about access, check before you proceed.

Minor revisions 2010

Printed by MWL, Pontypool.

ISBN: **978 1902302 69 0**